Sᴀᴄʀᴇᴅ Tʜʀᴇᴀᴅs

Forward

**A Special Exhibit by the
Sacred Threads 2015 Committee**

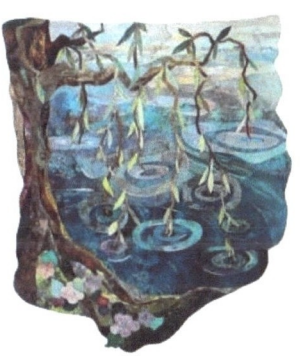

In these quilts, we express our interpretation of the word *forward* and what this means for each of us in our lives today.

Sacred Threads is known for our biennial exhibition of quilts exploring themes of spirituality, joy, grief, healing, inspiration, and peace/brotherhood.

Visit us online: www.sacredthreadsquilts.com

For more information about Sacred Threads, contact Lisa Ellis at lisa@ellisquilts.com.

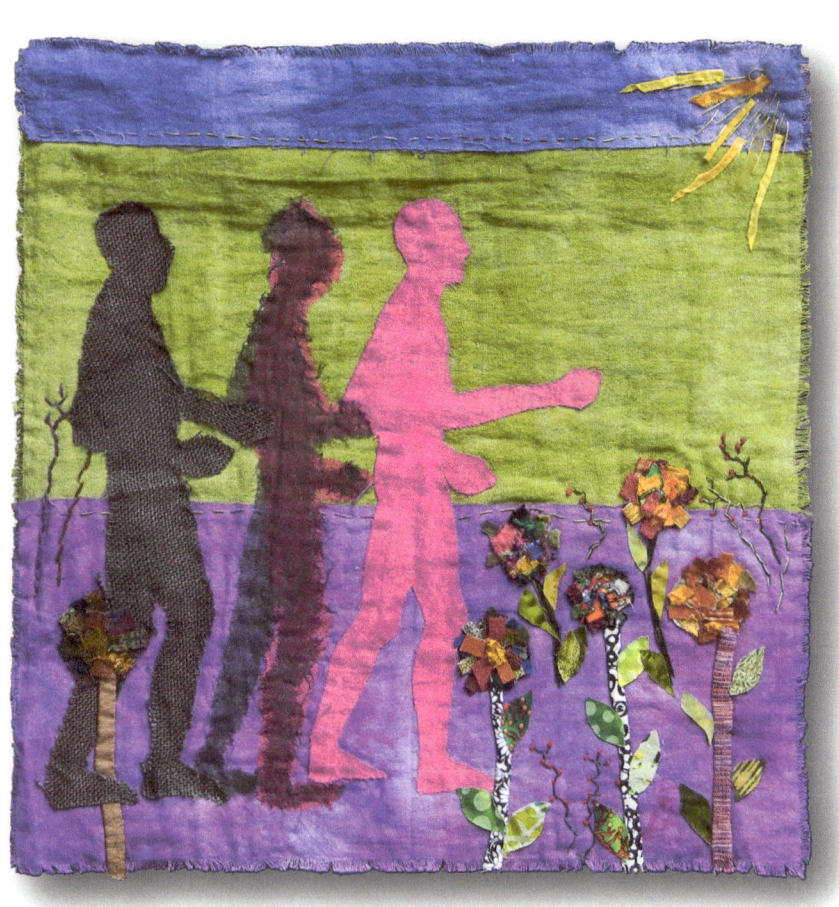

Annabel Ebersole
Williamsburg, VA

Forward Into Spring

My quilt speaks to the awakening of nature as we move from the gray, dreary winter into the light and delight of the first signs of spring. I am regularly renewing my spirit and my self through "beginning again." Recommitting to my self-discipline for studio, family and prayer time is how I move forward into renewal and the sharing of my gifts.

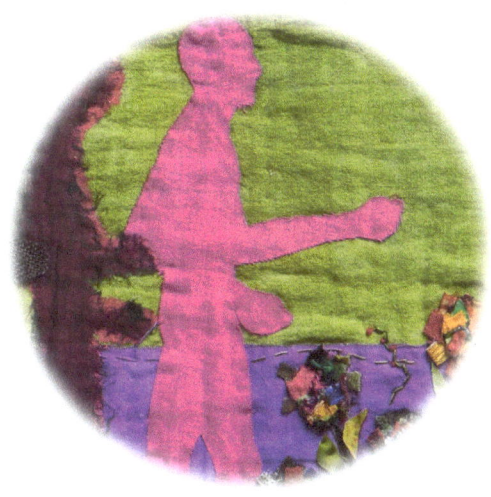

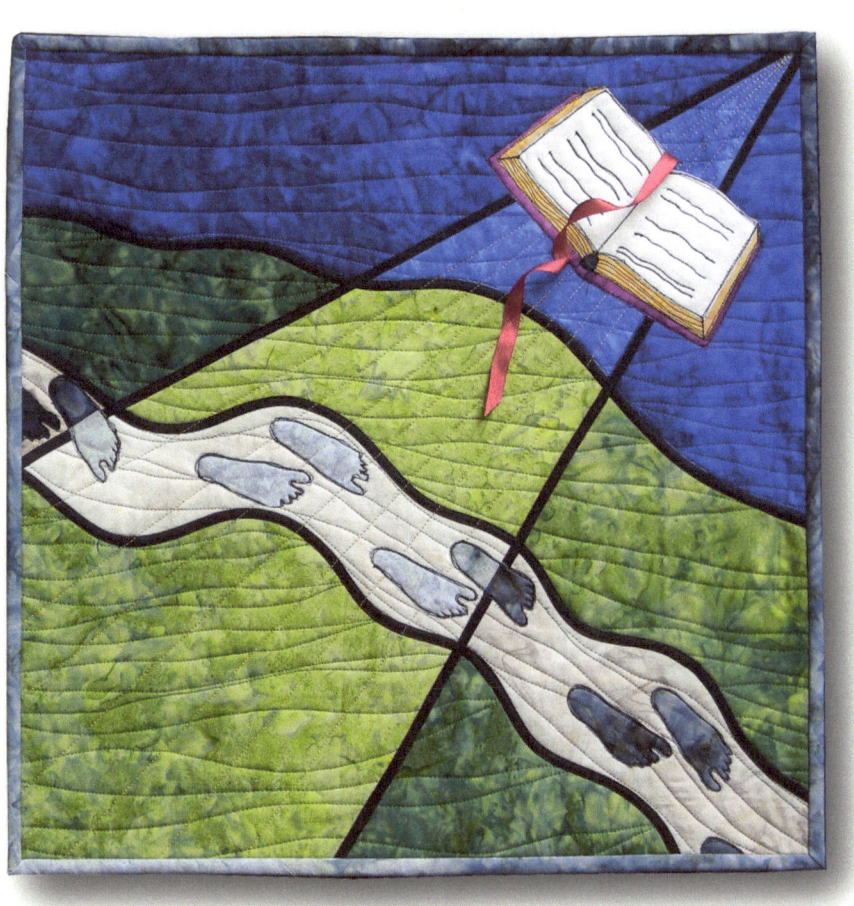

Lisa Ellis
Fairfax, VA
www.ellisquilts.com

Psalm 119:105

When trying to move forward with a decision, we just have to take one step at a time.

Psalm 119 promises that the Bible will shed light on our feet. It does not, however, illuminate the entire path ahead. So, we have to step out in faith.

"Your word is a lamp to my feet and a light to my path."
Psalm 119:105

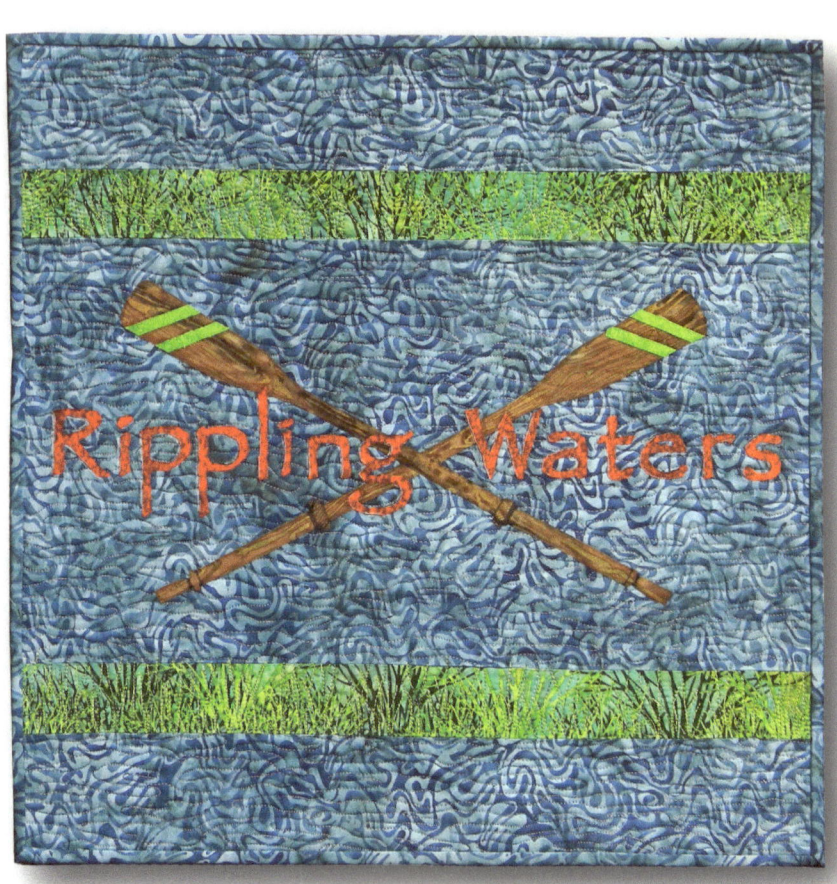

Sarah Enstminger
Ashburn, VA
www.studioatripplingwaters.com

Backward and Forward Are Sometimes the Same

Forward speaks to me of journeys, not any specific destination but rather a direction we move physically, mentally or emotionally through our life experiences. My decision to concentrate on an art vocation has shown me that to move forward, I have to go backward and capture the joy of creating that I experienced as a young artist. My time rowing crew in college was a physical reminder that backward energy is essential to success in forward movement. Backward and forward create the rhythms of daily life.

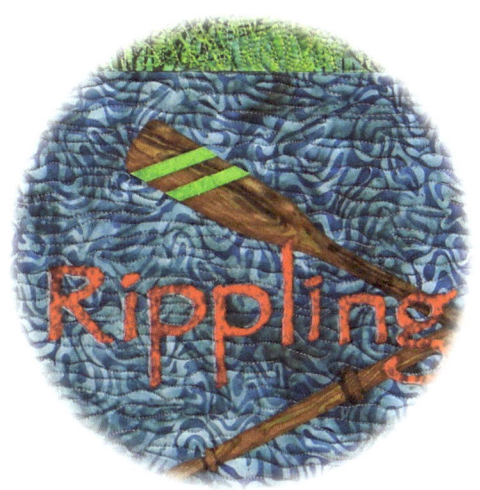

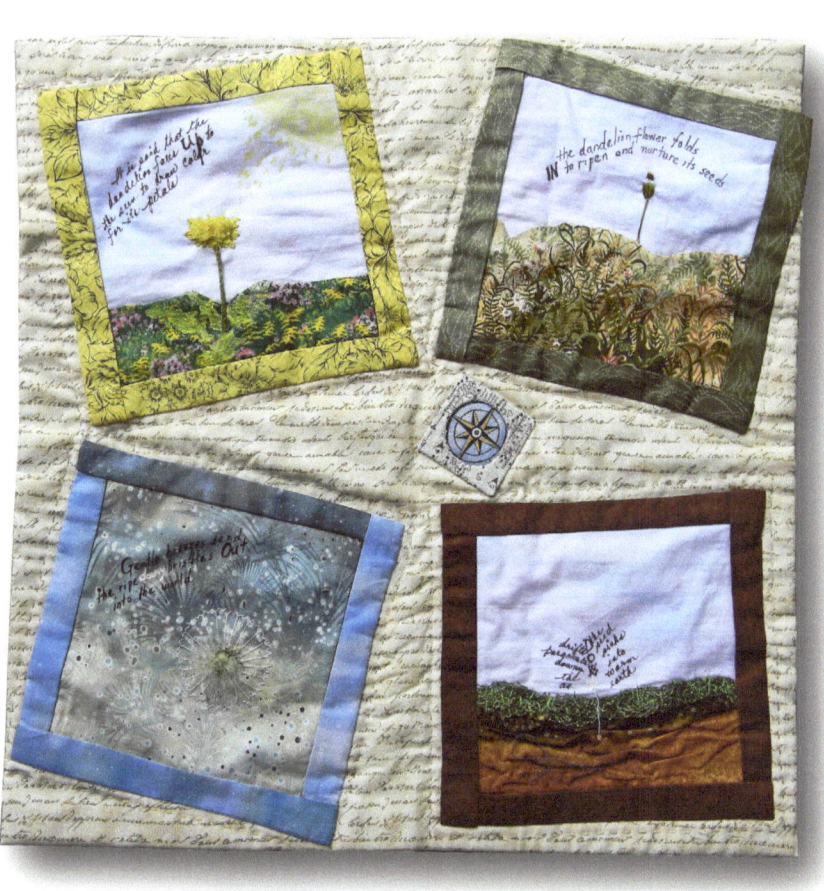

Elaine Evans
Middleburg, VA

Infinity

"Just where is 'Forward'?", demanded Curiosity Cat. "Why, it is the direction you are facing," replied Phoebe Philosopher.

The night sky full of stars ready for a wish, the road less traveled with hidden side paths, the corners of your mind seeking wisdom, the depths of your soul searching for wisdom, a book full of adventure, your heart singing a joyful noise, the sparkling depths of the sea, our choices are infinite.

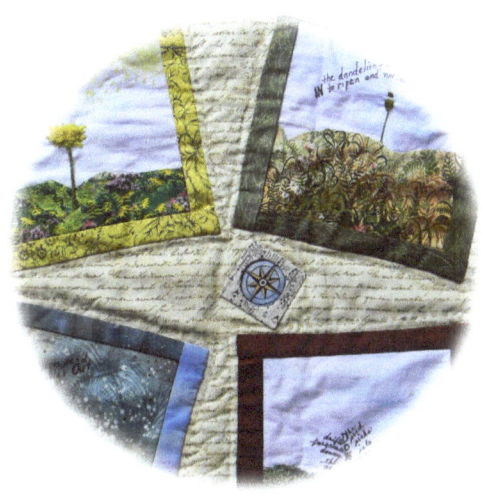

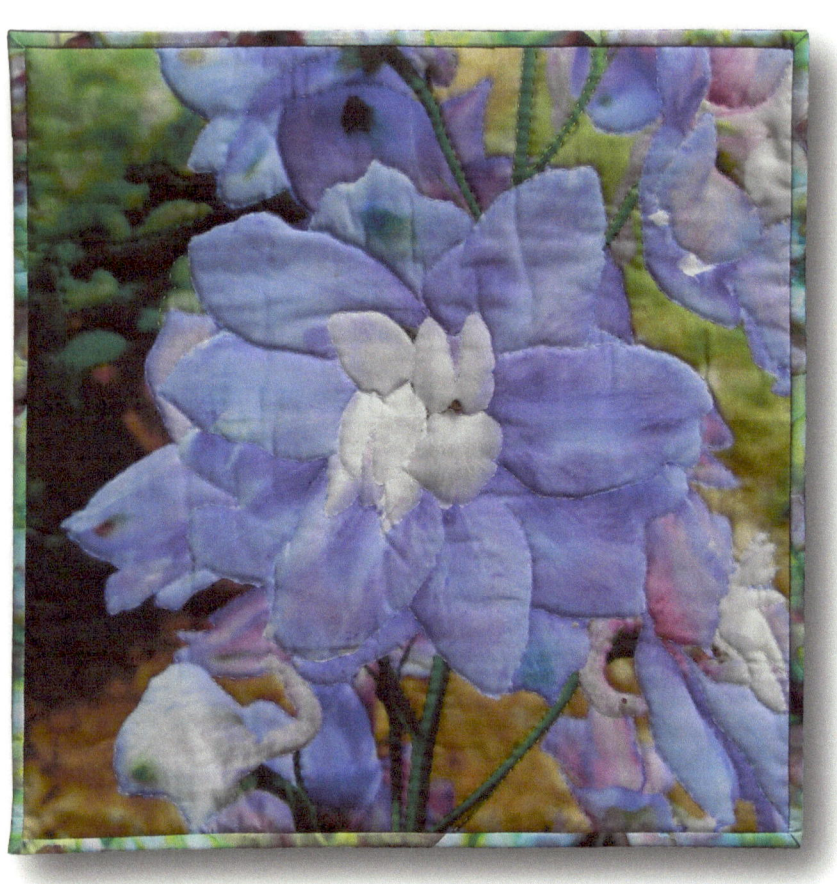

Sandi Goldman
Annandale, VA
www.quilts4celebration.com

Delphinium

My daily walks take me past many beautiful yards in my neighborhood. I can't help but stop and take photos of all the beauty I see. I'm always looking forward to the next flower I may find and the kind words of family and friends about how much they look forward to the photos I share on social media.

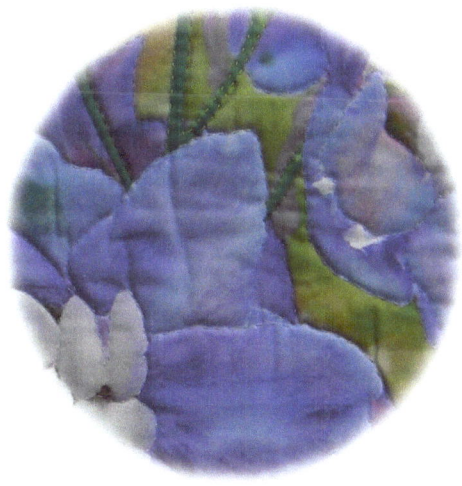

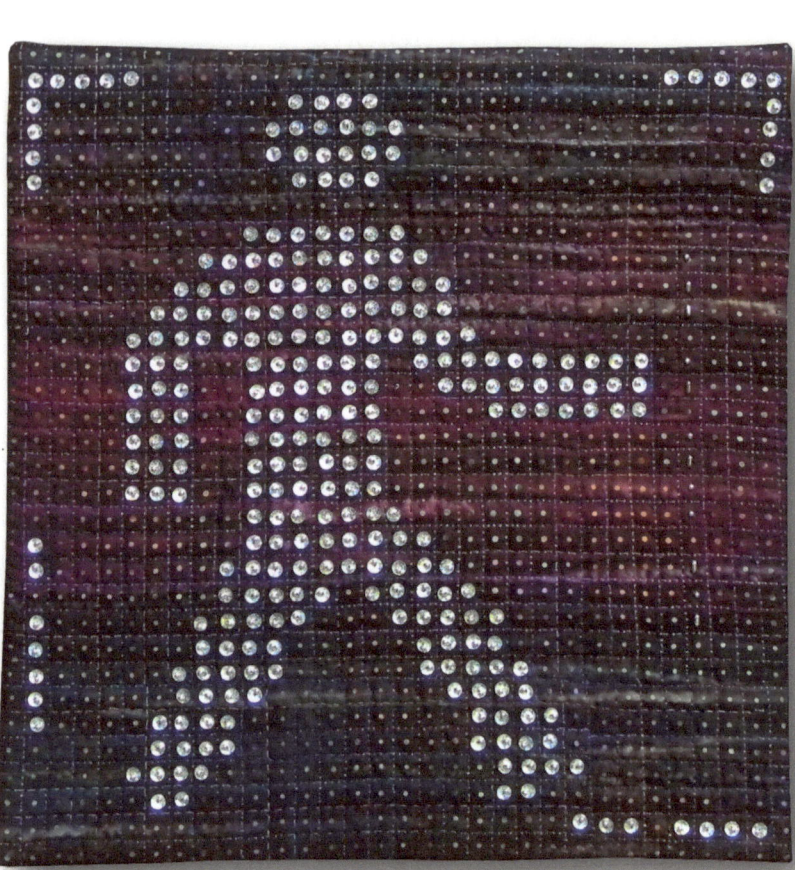

Barbara Hollinger
Vienna, VA

Walk!

I find myself at a crossroad in my life without clear direction as to which way to turn. I simply want to cry out "show me a sign"!

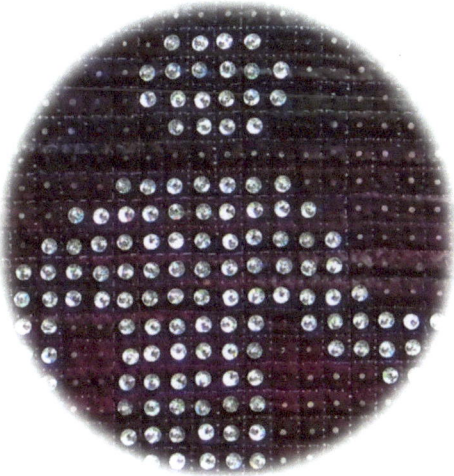

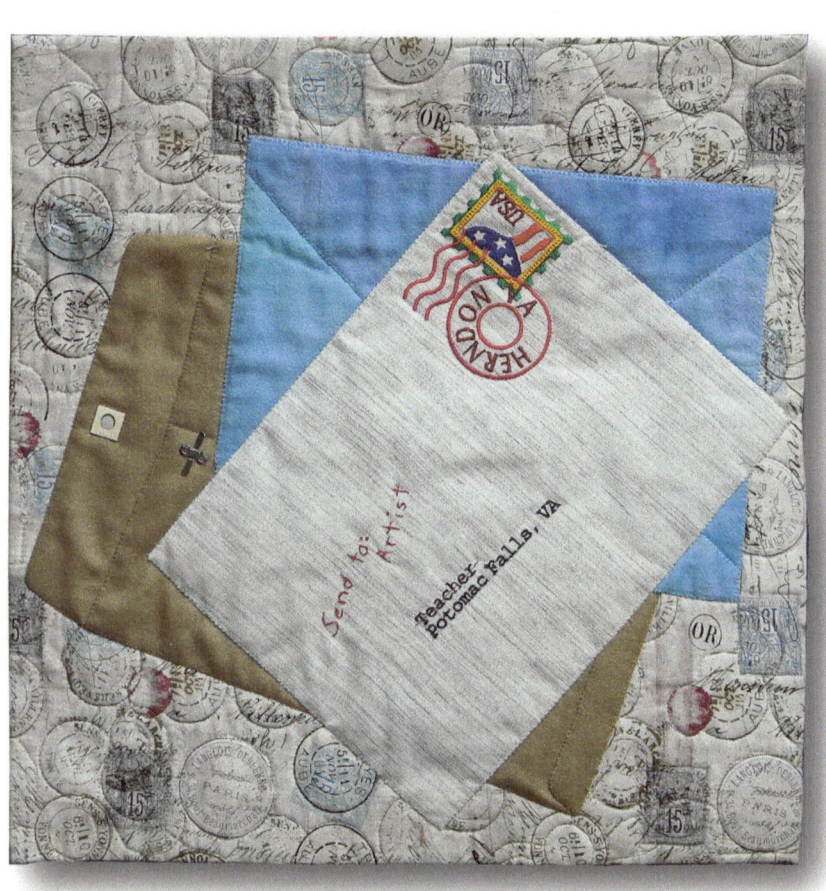

Susanne Jones
Sterling, VA

No Such Person - Please Forward

My identity, as an elementary school teacher, has changed. I worked with children most of my life and spent my spare time doing every conceivable kind of traditional needlework. No one called me an artist back then. When I retired from teaching in 2011, all of that changed. I found myself drawn to making art out of fabric and thread. My identity changed from Susanne, the teacher to Susanne, the artist. As I move forward, that is who I want to be.

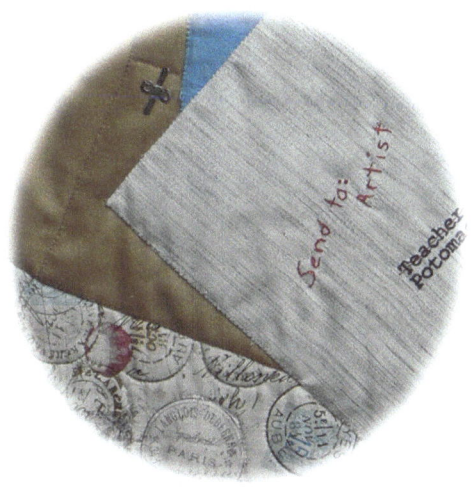

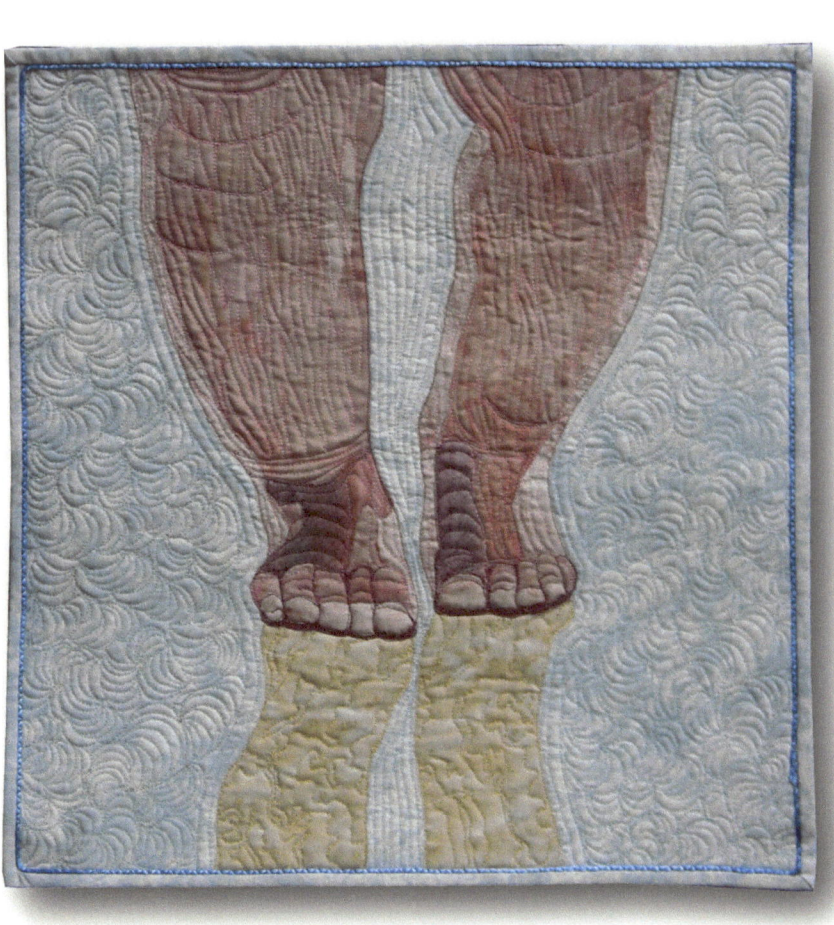

Bunnie Jordan
Vienna, VA
www.bunniejordan.com

Baby Steps

Baby's first steps are an exciting milestone that predicts future growth and independence. The persistence needed to master these solo steps also models tenacity and trust. Taking baby steps is a metaphor for a way to approach new beginnings or changes and challenges at any age. To move forward we start with a single baby step.

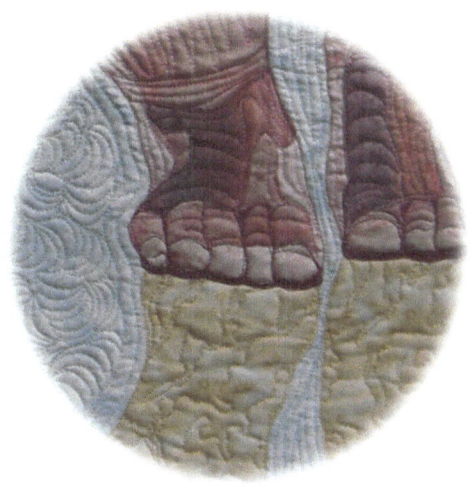

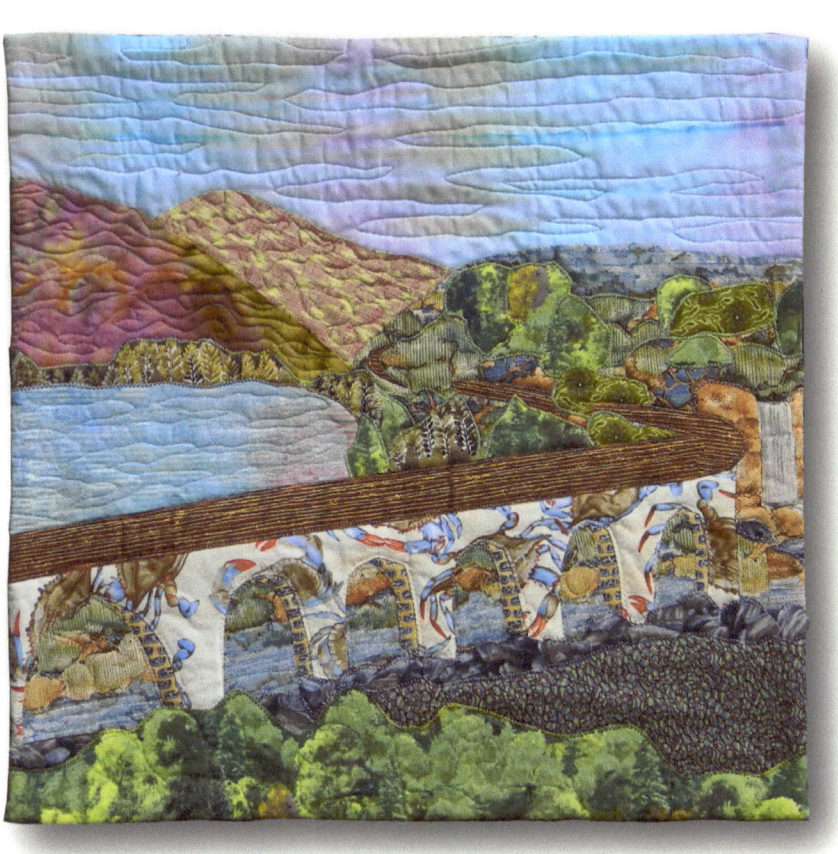

Lauren Kingsland
Sandy Spring, MD
www.laurenkingsland.com

Forward

This road traverses personal highs and lows while heading for an unknown vista in the future. The crabs in fabric of the bridge are about the fact that, although today I personally am well, the dance with cancer continues to be my teacher. This bridge is a metaphor for transcendence over and through obstacles and moving forward.

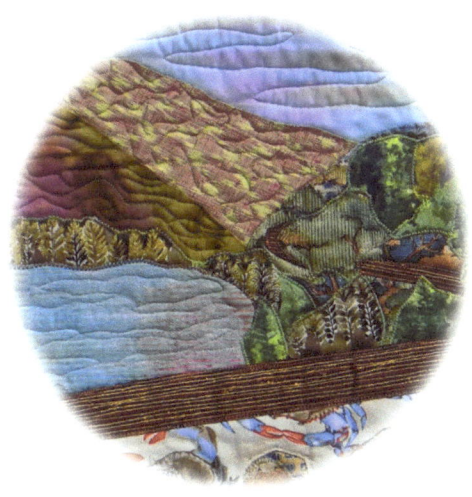

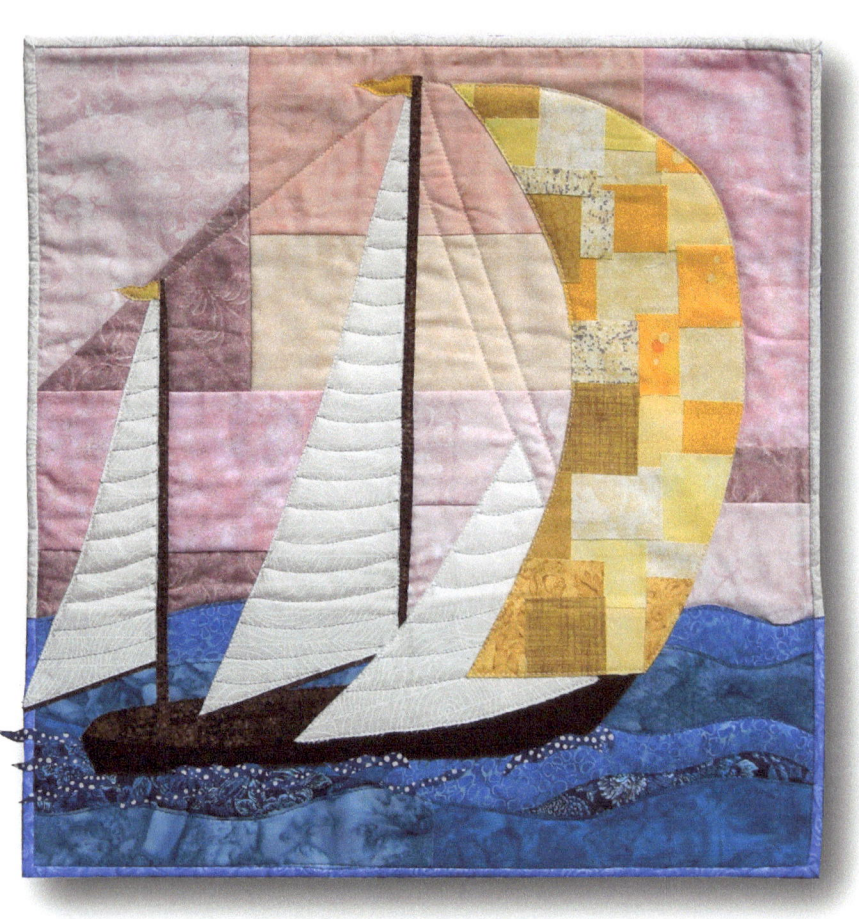

Audrey Lipps
Reston, VA

A Fresh Breeze

With a fresh breeze filling my sails, I'm off and running, ever moving forward. My challenge is to track the winds of change, staying open to unexpected shifts in direction that may signal a new way to proceed.

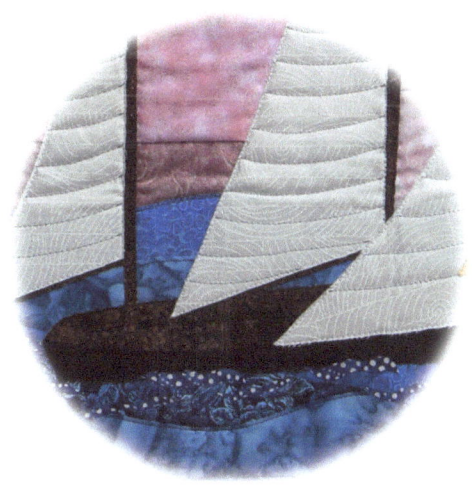

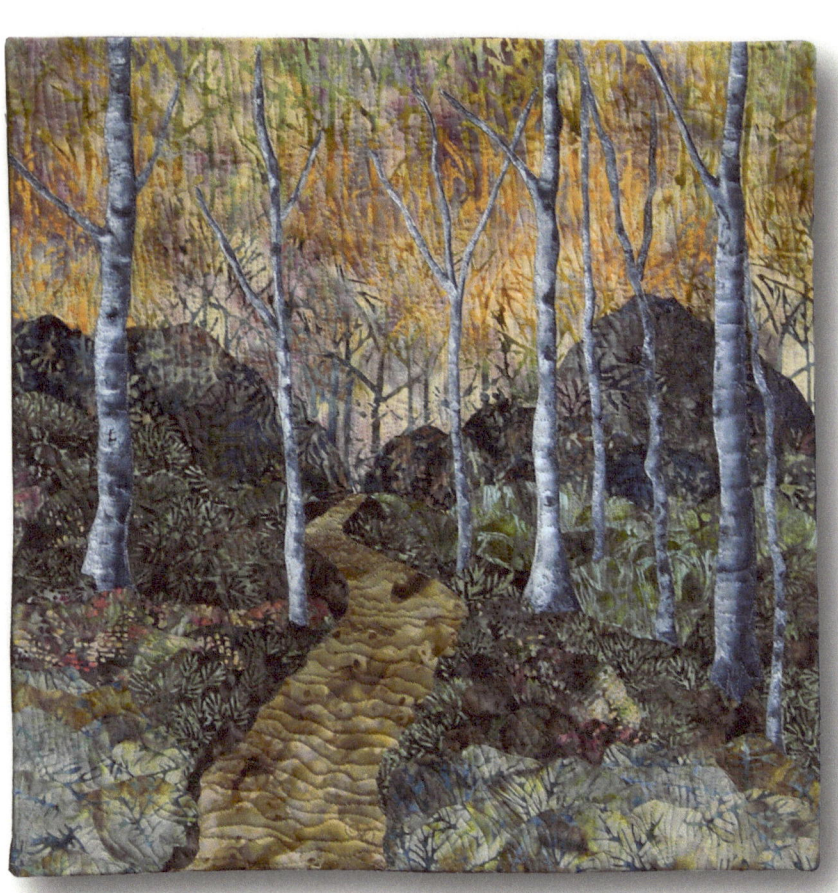

Vivian Milholen
South Riding, VA
www.studiothreads.blogspot.com

The Path

To reach our goals in life, we must keep moving forward and stay on our chosen path. Many things can distract us from following our heart's desire, such as losing confidence in our dream or trying to follow someone else's plan. We can stay on our path by listening to our inner being and seeking God's guidance.

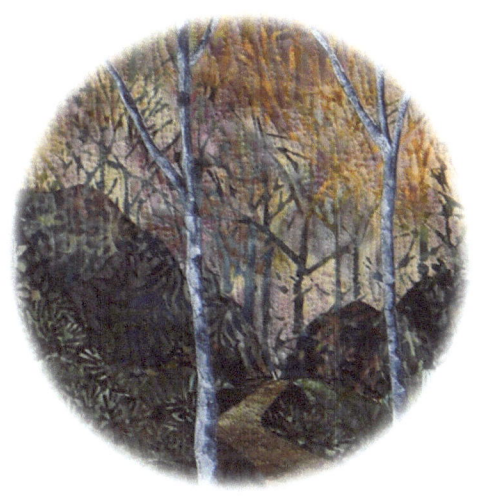

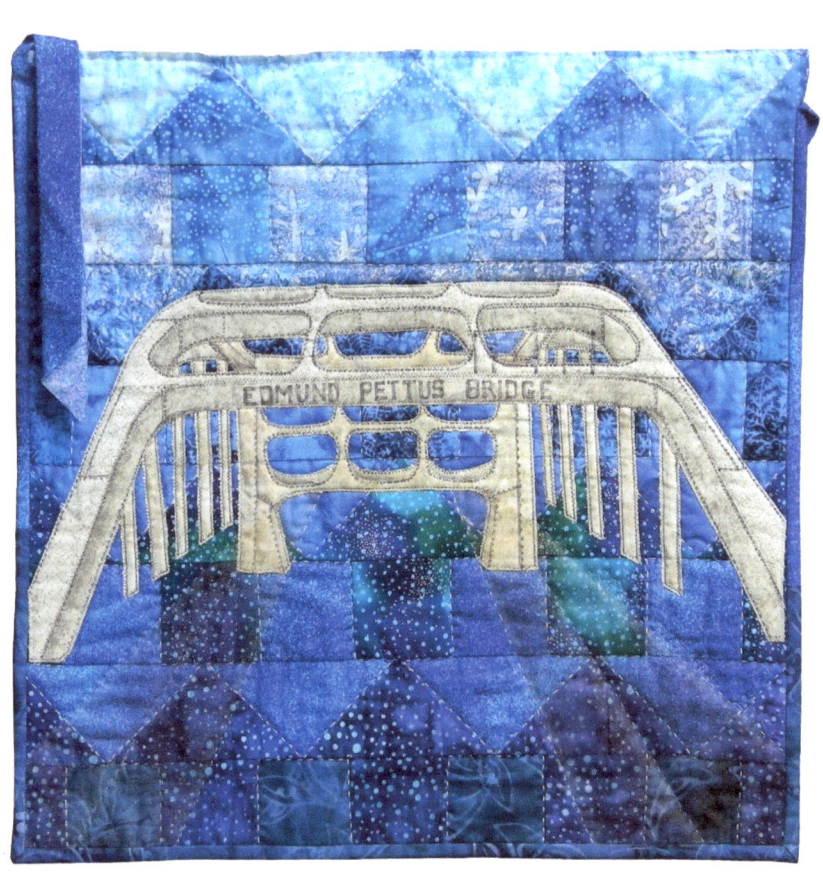

Carole A. Nicholas
Oakton, VA

Forward: We Are Not Yet Finished

The Edmund Pettus Bridge in Selma, Alabama marked the starting point of the March 7, 1965 Civil Rights March to Montgomery.

We have come a long way since that historical event, but our journey is still not completed. Just how far have we traveled? The background of my quilt is comprised of tessellated arrows; some point forward, others go the opposite way. The struggle for equality and justice is on-going, and like this quilt remains unfinished, a work-in-progress.

The title refers to words from a speech by President Barack Obama on   the 50th anniversary   of that March.

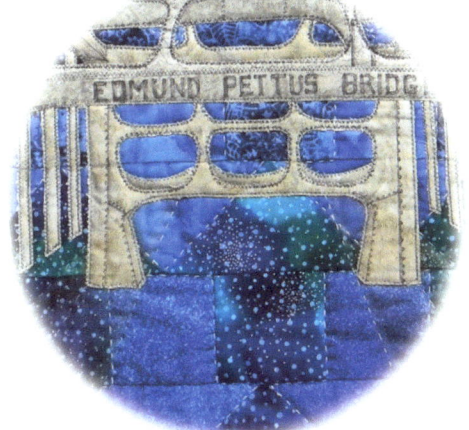

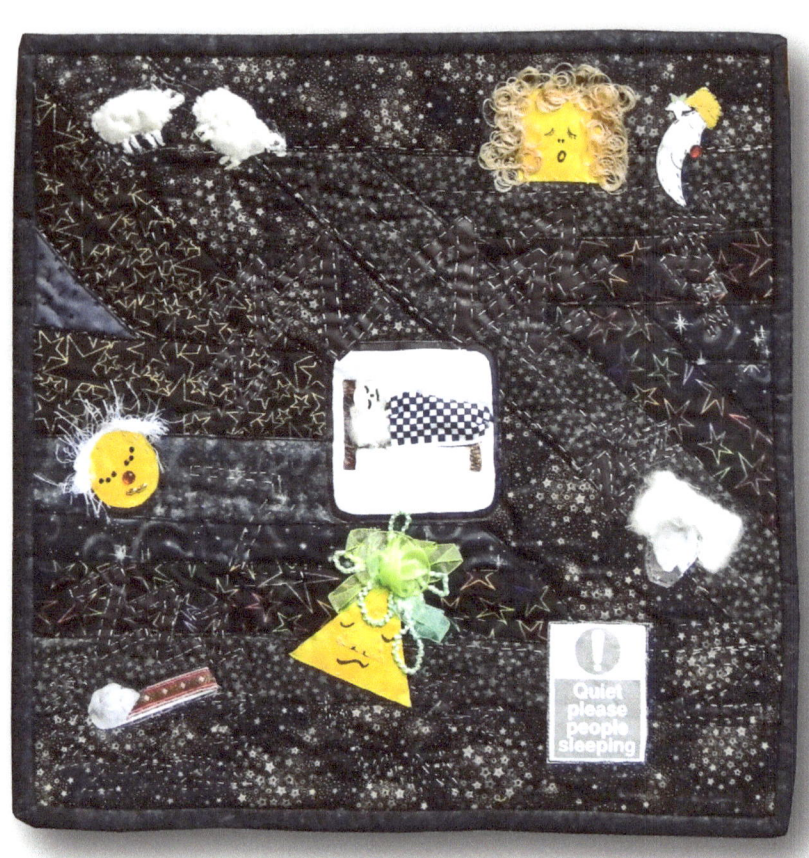

Starla Phelps
Alexandria, VA

THE GIFT . . . Sleep

As a result of RLS, sleep has been a challenge for me. I am presently undergoing some difficult challenges and new drugs. This Quilt Challenge Theme came at a perfect time for me. I LOOK "FORWARD" To SLEEP!!

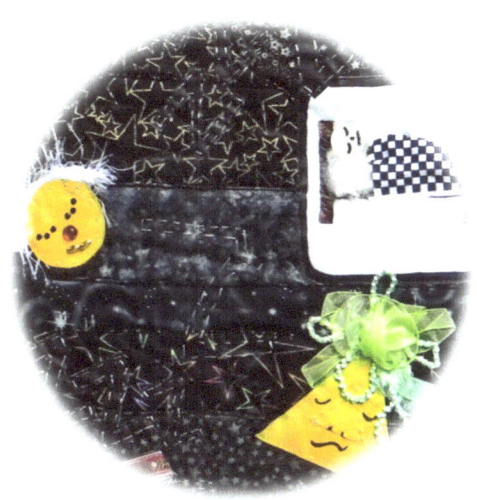

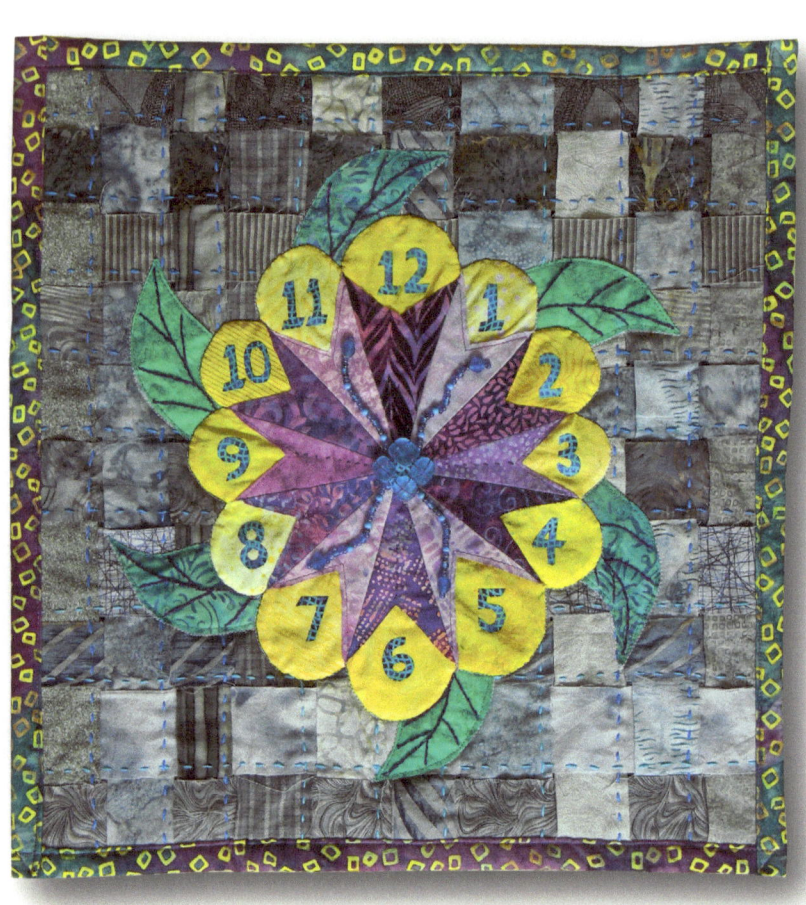

Shoshana Spiegel
Herndon, VA

Spring Forward

When daylight savings time comes in March, I willingly give up the hour of sleep and look forward to the miracle of spring. I am always amazed at how the green leaves and colorful blossoms emerge from the grayness of the seemingly endless winter. At my kitchen window I observe the weekly, then daily progress as the stark branches disappear beneath the bright foliage in the woods behind our home.

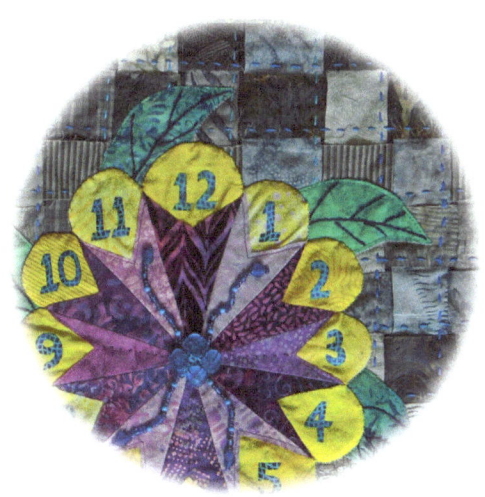

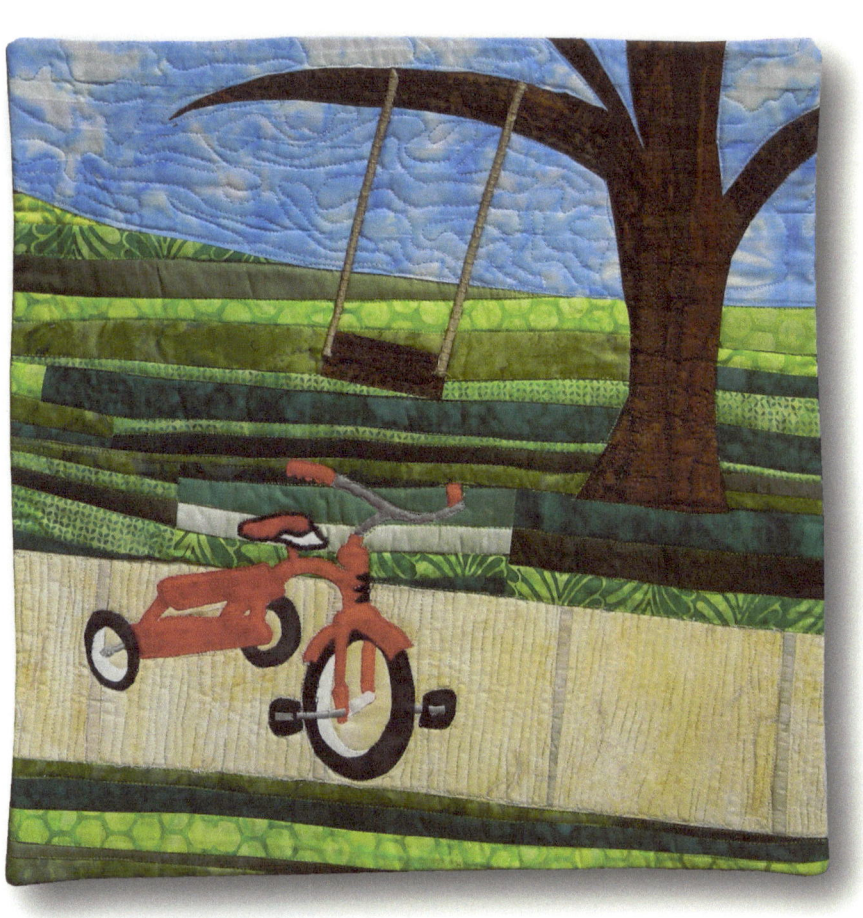

Anne Winchell
Oak Hill, VA

Child's Play

When a child is young they have their future to look forward to. They may want to grow up fast and move on to becoming an adult. As an adult we often look back and think with fondness of the friends we had and the games we played and think of how nice it would be to be young again.

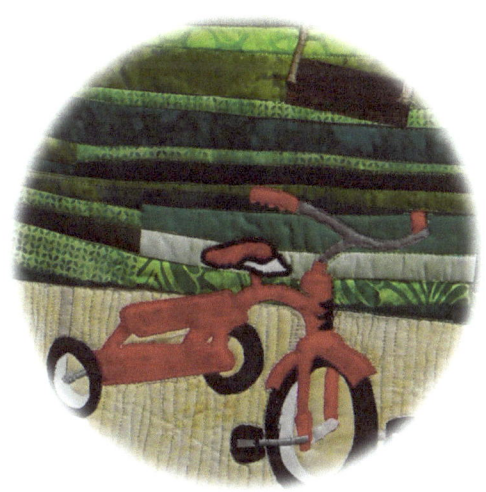

www.ingramcontent.com/pod-product-compliance
Lightning Source LLC
Chambersburg PA
CBHW040914180526
45159CB00010BA/3062